Wealth
Wise

A Comprehensive Guide to
Finance for College Students
and Youth

Asher Reed

Disclaimer: The information contained in this book is for general informational purposes only. The author and publisher make no representations or warranties of any kind, express or implied, about the completeness, accuracy, reliability, suitability, or availability of the information contained herein. Any reliance you place on such information is therefore strictly at your own risk.

Contents

Preface

Welcome to "Wealth Wise," a comprehensive guide designed to equip young individuals with essential knowledge and skills to navigate the world of finance. This book is specifically tailored to address the unique financial challenges and opportunities that youth face in today's ever-changing landscape.

Money management is a critical aspect of life, and establishing a strong foundation in financial literacy early on can have a profound impact on one's future.

In this book, I cover a wide range of topics, including money management basics, saving and investing, banking and financial services, earning and managing income, consumer skills and financial decision-making, understanding debt and managing credit, planning for the future, financial independence and entrepreneurship, and financial literacy beyond.

Each chapter offers relevant information, practical tips, case studies, and interactive exercises to engage and educate young readers. By actively participating in the exercises and reflecting on their financial journey, young individuals can take ownership of their financial well-being.

Whether you are a young adult just starting your financial journey or a college student seeking guidance on managing your finances, this book is here to provide you with the knowledge and skills necessary for financial success. I encourage you to read each chapter with an open mind, engage with the exercises, and apply the principles to your own life.

I hope that "Wealth Wise" becomes your go-to resource for financial knowledge and inspiration. May it empower you to make wise financial choices, cultivate healthy financial habits, and embark on a journey toward financial freedom and prosperity.

Sincerely,

Asher Reed

Chapter 1: The Basics of Money Management

Imagine this: You're standing in a candy store with a handful of coins. The colorful array of treats tempts you from every corner, but you quickly realize that you can't have them all. You have to make choices. How will you spend your limited coins? Will you go for your favorite candy, or will you save them for a special occasion? The decisions you make in that moment reflect the value you place on each candy and the understanding that every choice has consequences.

This is just a small glimpse into the world of money and its significance in our lives. Money is more than just pieces of paper or numbers on a screen. It is a powerful tool that allows us to fulfill our needs and desires, create opportunities, and shape our future. But to harness its power effectively, we must first understand its value.

Opportunity cost: It is a concept that highlights the trade-offs we face when making financial choices. Think about it: when you spend your money on one thing, you're giving up the opportunity to spend it on something else. This concept extends beyond candy stores; it applies to all aspects of life. By understanding the concept of opportunity cost, you'll be better equipped to make choices that align with your priorities and long-term goals.

Time value of money: Time has a remarkable effect on our finances. When you save and invest your money wisely, it has the potential to grow over time through the magic of compound interest. This means that the sooner you start saving and investing, the more your money can work for you, multiplying and expanding your financial resources.

Get ready to embark on an exciting adventure of financial discovery. By mastering the basics of money management, you will gain the confidence and skills to navigate the complex world of finance, laying the groundwork for a prosperous and fulfilling future. So, let's dive in and unlock the secrets to mastering the value of money, setting financial goals, and building a solid foundation for your financial journey. Your future self will thank you for it!

Practical Tip: Reflect on your financial decisions and consider the opportunity costs involved. Think about how you can make choices that align with your goals and values.

Setting Financial Goals

Setting financial goals gives you direction and purpose for managing your money. Here's how to establish meaningful financial goals:

Setting financial goals is like setting a destination on a map. It helps guide your financial journey and gives you something to work towards. By defining your goals, you create a clear vision of what you want to achieve, and the steps needed to get there. Let's explore different types of financial goals:

Short-Term Goals: These goals are achievable within a year or less. Short-term goals are often smaller, more immediate targets that you can accomplish relatively quickly. Examples of short-term goals may include saving for a new phone, buying a concert ticket, or paying off a small debt. These goals provide a sense of accomplishment and motivate you to continue working towards your larger aspirations.

Medium-Term Goals: These goals typically take between one to five years to achieve. They require more planning and dedication than short-term goals but are still within reach. Medium-term goals can encompass a wide range of objectives depending on your individual circumstances and ambitions. Examples may include saving for a car, funding a study abroad program, or starting a small business. These goals require consistent effort and a focus on long-term planning.

Long-Term Goals: Long-term goals extend beyond five years into the future. They often require significant commitment and may shape the course of your entire life. Long-term goals are crucial for building financial security and achieving major milestones. Examples include saving for college, buying a house, or building a retirement fund. These goals require patience, discipline, and a long-term perspective, but they offer substantial rewards and provide a roadmap for your financial success.

When setting financial goals, it's essential to make them specific, measurable, achievable, relevant, and time-bound (SMART). This approach ensures that your goals are well-defined and actionable. By breaking down your long-term goals into smaller, manageable steps, you create a roadmap that leads to success.

Remember, financial goals are unique to each individual. They should reflect your values, priorities, and dreams. Take the time to identify what truly matters to you and align your goals with your aspirations. Your financial goals will act as a compass, guiding you towards the life you envision.

As we progress through this book, we will explore various strategies to achieve your financial goals. From creating effective budgeting plans to maximizing your savings and exploring investment opportunities, each step will bring you closer to realizing your dreams. So, let's continue this journey and learn how to set meaningful financial goals that inspire and empower you to take charge of your financial future.

Case Study: Meet Sarah, an ambitious and determined young woman with a deep passion for environmental science. From a young age, she dreamt of attending college to study this field and make a positive impact on the world around her. However, like many aspiring students, Sarah faced a significant hurdle: the financial cost of higher education.

Undeterred by the challenges ahead, Sarah set a financial goal for herself: to save $20,000 over the next four years to cover tuition fees, books, and living expenses. She understood that achieving her dream would require careful planning, discipline, and perseverance.

Sarah began her journey by creating a budget that accounted for her income and expenses. She meticulously tracked her spending, making conscious choices to prioritize her savings goals. By scrutinizing her expenses, she discovered areas where she could cut back, such as reducing eating out and finding affordable alternatives for entertainment.

Recognizing the importance of generating additional income, Sarah sought out a part-time job that would fit around her studies. She found a position at a local café, allowing her to earn extra money while maintaining a balance with her academic commitments. Sarah dedicated herself to her job, working diligently and saving a significant portion of her income each month.

As Sarah progressed through her college journey, she remained focused on her financial goal. She avoided unnecessary expenses and embraced frugal living without sacrificing her overall well-being. She took advantage of discounts, shopped for used textbooks, and explored scholarship opportunities to lighten the financial burden.

Sarah's determination and unwavering commitment paid off. Through her consistent efforts and smart financial choices, she successfully saved the $20,000 needed for her college education. Sarah's dream of attending college to study environmental science became a reality, thanks to her disciplined savings plan and steadfast dedication.

But Sarah's journey didn't stop there. Armed with her degree and a solid financial foundation, she continued to manage her money wisely, avoiding unnecessary debt and making informed investment decisions. Sarah's financial literacy and responsible financial habits served as a springboard for her future success and financial well-being.

Sarah's story serves as an inspiring example of how setting clear financial goals, creating a budget, and making smart choices can pave the way for achieving lifelong dreams. Her determination, perseverance, and financial discipline enabled her to overcome obstacles and transform her aspirations into reality.

As you embark on your own financial journey, remember Sarah's story. Let it fuel your determination and remind you that with careful planning, dedication, and a focus on your goals, you too can turn your dreams into achievements. So, set your sights high, create a roadmap for your financial success, and make your own inspiring story a reality.

Interactive Exercise: Create Your Financial Goals Take a moment to brainstorm your financial goals. Write down three short-term goals, two medium-term goals, and one long-

term goal. Think about why these goals are important to you and how achieving them will enhance your life.

Creating a Budget

A budget is a tool that helps you manage your income and expenses. It allows you to prioritize your spending, avoid overspending, and allocate funds towards your goals. Here's how to create a budget:

Creating a budget is like having a roadmap for your money. It provides structure and guidance, ensuring that you're making conscious choices about how you spend and save. By creating a budget, you gain control over your financial resources and maximize their potential. Let's explore the steps to create an effective budget:

1. **Track Your Income:** Begin by listing all your sources of income. This may include allowances, part-time jobs, or any other form of financial support you receive. By understanding how much money you have coming in, you can better plan and allocate your funds.

2. **Identify Your Expenses:** Categorize your expenses into fixed and variable categories. Fixed expenses are those that remain relatively consistent each month, such as rent, utilities, or insurance payments. Variable expenses, on the other hand, fluctuate and may include entertainment, dining out, or personal care. Don't forget to include savings as an expense category. It's important to prioritize saving for future goals and emergencies.

3. **Set Spending Limits:** Now that you have a clear picture of your income and expenses, it's time to allocate funds to each category. Set spending limits based on your priorities and financial goals. Consider what is essential and where you can make adjustments. It's crucial to ensure that your income covers your expenses and leaves room for savings.

4. **Monitor and Adjust:** Your budget isn't a one-time exercise—it requires ongoing attention. Regularly review

your budget and track your actual spending against your planned allocations. This helps you identify any areas where you may be overspending or where you have extra funds that could be reallocated. Adjust your budget as needed to stay on track and make improvements.

Creating a budget may seem daunting at first, but it's a powerful tool for financial empowerment. It enables you to make intentional decisions about how you use your money, align your spending with your values, and work towards your financial goals.

Interactive Exercise: Create Your Budget Using a budgeting template or app, create your own budget. Allocate percentages or amounts to different expense categories, ensuring that you prioritize savings. Track your expenses for a month and assess how well you stick to your budget.

Developing Smart Spending Habits

Developing smart spending habits is crucial for maintaining a healthy financial lifestyle. Here are some strategies to help you make wise spending decisions:

Developing smart spending habits is like building a strong foundation for your financial well-being. It involves making conscious choices about how you allocate your resources and ensuring that your spending aligns with your long-term goals. By cultivating smart spending habits, you can achieve financial stability and maximize the value of your money. Let's explore some strategies:

1. **Differentiate Between Needs and Wants:** It's essential to distinguish between essential needs and discretionary wants. Needs include fundamental necessities such as food, shelter, and education. Wants, on the other hand, encompass desires for non-essential items like entertainment, fashion, or luxury goods. Prioritize spending on needs, ensuring that they

are met first, and limit indulgence in wants. This practice helps you allocate your resources effectively and prevents overspending on non-essential items.

2. **Practice Delayed Gratification:** One of the keys to smart spending is avoiding impulse purchases. Instead of giving in to immediate desires, practice delayed gratification. Give yourself time to consider whether a purchase aligns with your goals and values. This allows you to evaluate its importance and necessity in the context of your overall financial plan. By consciously delaying purchases, you can avoid buyer's remorse and make more thoughtful spending decisions.

3. **Comparison Shopping:** When making purchases, it's important to compare prices, quality, and reviews. Take the time to research different options and consider alternatives before finalizing a purchase. By engaging in comparison shopping, you ensure that you get the best value for your money. This habit

allows you to make informed decisions, avoid overpaying, and make purchases that align with your budget and priorities.

4. **Avoid Lifestyle Inflation:** Lifestyle inflation refers to increasing your spending as your income increases. It's tempting to upgrade your lifestyle and indulge in more luxurious purchases as your financial situation improves. However, it's important to resist this temptation and instead focus on saving and investing more for the future. By avoiding lifestyle inflation, you can allocate a larger portion of your income towards your financial goals, such as saving for emergencies, investing for long-term growth, or achieving other significant milestones.

Developing smart spending habits requires self-discipline and a commitment to long-term financial success. As you progress through this book, you will gain valuable insights into managing your spending effectively. From budgeting techniques to tips for curbing impulse buying, each step will empower you to make smart spending choices and optimize your financial resources.

Case Study: Meet Jake, an avid video game enthusiast who has a dream of owning his own car. However, he realizes that his love for video games often leads him to overspend and neglect his long-term financial goals. Determined to change his habits and prioritize saving, Jake devises a plan to adjust his spending and achieve his dream of owning a car.

Jake starts by taking a closer look at his spending patterns and identifies video game purchases as a significant drain on his finances. He realizes that by cutting back on his video game expenses, he can redirect that money towards saving for his dream car. With newfound determination, Jake sets a goal for himself to limit his video game purchases and saves the money he would have otherwise spent.

To achieve his goal, Jake implements several strategies:

1. *Setting a Budget: Jake creates a budget that allows him to allocate a specific*

amount of money each month towards his car savings. He considers his income, expenses, and other financial obligations, ensuring that he can comfortably save without compromising other important aspects of his life.

2. *Prioritizing Long-Term Goals: Jake reminds himself of the importance of his long-term goal—buying a car. He keeps this goal in mind whenever he is tempted to make impulsive video game purchases. By shifting his mindset and focusing on the bigger picture, Jake strengthens his commitment to saving for his dream car.*

3. *Delayed Gratification: Jake practices delayed gratification, resisting the immediate desire to purchase the latest video game releases. Instead, he puts off buying new games and redirects that money towards his car savings. This conscious choice allows him to accumulate more significant savings over time.*

4. *Exploring Affordable Alternatives:*
   Recognizing his love for gaming, Jake
   explores affordable alternatives to
   purchasing new games at full price. He
   looks for sales, discounts, or even
   considers borrowing games from friends
   or renting them. By finding cost-effective
   ways to enjoy his hobby, Jake reduces his
   expenses while still indulging in his
   passion.

Through his commitment to smart spending adjustments, Jake successfully accumulates enough savings to purchase his dream car. The sacrifices he made in limiting his video game purchases were outweighed by the fulfillment of achieving a long-term goal and the pride of financial responsibility.

Jake's story serves as a powerful reminder of the importance of aligning spending habits with long-term goals. By making conscious choices, setting priorities, and practicing delayed gratification, he was able to redirect his resources and turn his dream into a reality.

Interactive Exercise: Evaluate Your Spending Habits Take a critical look at your spending habits. Identify one area where you tend to overspend or make impulsive purchases. Develop a plan to curb this habit and redirect the money saved towards a financial goal.

Chapter 2: Saving and Investing

Saving money is a fundamental financial habit that allows you to build a safety net, meet financial goals, and handle unexpected expenses. Here are some key reasons why saving is important:

Saving money is not just a good practice; it is a powerful tool that can transform your financial life. By setting aside a portion of your income, you create a safety net, work towards your long-term goals, and gain the freedom to make choices that align with your aspirations. Let's explore some compelling reasons why saving is important:

1. **Emergency Fund:** Life is full of uncertainties, and having an emergency fund is like having a financial safety net. It provides a cushion for unforeseen events such as medical emergencies, car repairs, or sudden job loss. By saving and building an

emergency fund, you can navigate these unexpected expenses without relying on credit or falling into debt. Aim to save at least three to six months' worth of living expenses, as this will provide you with a sense of security and peace of mind.

2. **Financial Independence:** Saving money empowers you to achieve financial independence. It means having the freedom to make choices based on your preferences and values rather than being limited by financial constraints. With a solid savings foundation, you can pursue your dreams, start a business, or retire comfortably. Saving allows you to take control of your financial future and reduces the reliance on external sources for financial support.

3. **Long-Term Goals:** We all have dreams and aspirations that require financial resources to fulfill. Whether it's buying a house, funding education, or traveling the world, saving plays a vital

role in making progress toward your long-term goals. By consistently saving and accumulating funds, you can turn your dreams into reality. Saving also enables you to take advantage of opportunities that may arise along the way, such as investment opportunities or career changes.

4. **Financial Security:** Saving provides a sense of financial security and stability. It acts as a buffer against unexpected financial challenges, allowing you to weather economic downturns or personal setbacks more effectively. By building your savings, you are better equipped to handle life's uncertainties and maintain your financial well-being even in challenging times.

Incorporating saving into your financial habits is a wise decision that pays off in the long run. It requires discipline, commitment, and a willingness to make conscious choices about how you allocate your resources. As you progress through this book, you will learn valuable strategies and techniques to optimize your saving habits and make the most of your financial resources.

Interactive Exercise: Set a Savings Goal Identify a short-term savings goal, such as saving for a new gadget or a concert ticket. Determine how much you need to save and calculate how long it will take to reach your goal by saving a specific amount each month. Monitor your progress along the way.

Building an Emergency Fund

An emergency fund is a crucial component of financial stability. Here's how you can build and maintain an emergency fund:

Building an emergency fund is like constructing a strong financial safety net. It provides you with a sense of security and helps you navigate unexpected financial challenges without derailing your progress toward your goals. Here are some key steps to building and maintaining an emergency fund:

1. **Determine Your Target:** To start building an emergency fund, calculate your monthly living expenses. Take into account essential expenses such as

rent, utilities, groceries, transportation, and any other necessary costs. Multiply this monthly amount by the number of months you want to save for, typically three to six months. This will give you your target emergency fund amount. Knowing the target provides you with a clear goal to work towards.

2. **Start Small:** Building an emergency fund can seem overwhelming, especially if you're starting from scratch. However, remember that every journey begins with a single step. Start by saving a small amount regularly, even if it's just a few dollars each week. The key is consistency. Over time, gradually increase the amount you save as your financial situation allows. Small contributions add up, and before you know it, you'll be well on your way to reaching your emergency fund target.

3. **Protect Your Fund:** Once you start building your emergency fund, it's essential to protect it. Keep your emergency fund in a separate savings

account that is easily accessible but not readily spent. This separation helps ensure that the money remains dedicated to emergencies only. Consider setting up automatic transfers from your checking account to your emergency fund to make saving effortless and consistent. Resist the temptation to dip into the fund for non-emergency expenses, as doing so can undermine its purpose.

4. **Maintain and Replenish:** Building an emergency fund is not a one-time task. It requires ongoing maintenance. Life circumstances may change, expenses may increase, or emergencies may arise that deplete your fund. Regularly review your emergency fund and make adjustments as necessary. If you need to use some or all of the funds for an emergency, make replenishing the fund a priority once the situation has stabilized. Aim to restore it to the target amount as soon as possible.

Interactive Exercise: Consider opening a high-yield savings account or a money market account to earn a higher interest rate on your emergency fund.

Case Study: Meet Olivia, a proactive and financially responsible individual who understands the importance of building an emergency fund. Olivia's commitment to saving a portion of her income each month proves to be a wise decision when she encounters an unforeseen expense.

Olivia diligently saves a portion of her income each month with the specific goal of building an emergency fund. She understands that life can be unpredictable, and having a financial safety net is essential. After six months of consistent saving, Olivia finds herself facing unexpected car repairs that require a significant amount of money.

Fortunately, Olivia's foresight and dedication to saving pay off. Thanks to her emergency fund, she has the necessary funds to cover the expense without resorting to credit cards or loans. This not only provides her with immediate relief but also safeguards her financial well-being in the long run.

By relying on her emergency fund instead of incurring additional debt, Olivia demonstrates the true value of this financial safety net. She can handle unexpected situations without jeopardizing her financial stability or derailing her progress toward her other financial goals.

Olivia's story serves as a powerful reminder of the importance of building and maintaining an emergency fund. It highlights the peace of mind and financial resilience that come with having a dedicated fund to handle unexpected expenses.

As you embark on your own financial journey, let Olivia's experience inspire you to prioritize building your emergency fund. By consistently saving and being prepared for unforeseen circumstances, you can protect yourself from financial stress and maintain control over your financial future.

Introduction to Investing

Investing is the process of allocating money with the expectation of generating income or capital appreciation over time. While saving focuses on preserving money, investing aims to grow it. Here's why investing is important:

Investing is a crucial component of a well-rounded financial strategy. It offers the potential to grow your wealth and achieve long-term financial goals. Let's explore some key reasons why investing is important:

1. **Wealth Building:** Investing provides an opportunity to grow your wealth over time. While saving money is essential, it may not be enough to outpace inflation, which erodes the purchasing power of your savings. By investing, you can potentially generate higher returns that surpass the rate of inflation. This can be particularly valuable when working towards long-term financial goals, such as saving for retirement or purchasing a home.

2. **Compound Interest:** One of the most powerful concepts in investing is compound interest. By investing early and consistently, you can harness the exponential growth potential of compound interest. This occurs when

your earnings generate additional earnings, leading to a snowball effect over time. The earlier you start investing, the more time your investments have to benefit from the compounding effect. This can significantly accelerate the growth of your wealth and help you achieve your financial goals faster.

3. **Diversification:** Investing in a diverse range of assets is key to managing risk and increasing the likelihood of earning positive returns. Diversification involves spreading your investments across different asset classes, such as stocks, bonds, real estate, and commodities. By diversifying, you reduce the impact of any single investment on your overall portfolio. This helps mitigate potential losses and ensures that your investment returns are not overly reliant on the performance of a single asset or sector.

4. **Financial Independence:** Investing plays a crucial role in achieving

financial independence. By consistently growing your wealth through smart investment decisions, you can reduce reliance on active income from employment. Investments that generate passive income, such as dividends, interest, or rental income, can provide a steady stream of cash flow that supports your financial needs. Ultimately, this financial independence gives you greater flexibility and freedom to pursue your passions, travel, or retire comfortably.

Investing, however, comes with risks, and it's important to educate yourself and make informed decisions. Throughout this book, we will explore various investment strategies, risk management techniques, and tips to help you navigate the world of investing successfully.

Interactive Exercise: Explore Investment Options Research different investment options, such as stocks, bonds, mutual funds, and real estate. Create a list of pros and cons for each investment type, considering factors like risk, return potential, and liquidity.

Exploring Investment Options: There are various investment options available to young investors. Let's explore a few common investment avenues:

- **Stocks:** Investing in individual stocks allows you to own shares of a company. Research companies, analyze their financial health, and consider long-term growth potential.

Pros:

1. Potential for high returns: Stocks have the potential for significant capital appreciation, especially when invested in well-performing companies.

2. Ownership and voting rights: As a shareholder, you have ownership in the company and may have the right to vote on important company decisions.

3. Flexibility: Stocks offer the flexibility to buy and sell shares based on market conditions or your investment goals.

4. Dividends: Some stocks pay dividends, which are a portion of the company's profits distributed to shareholders.

Cons:

1. Volatility and risk: Stocks can be subject to price fluctuations, and their value can vary significantly in the short term. There is always the risk of losing money when investing in individual stocks.

2. Research and analysis: Investing in stocks requires thorough research and analysis of company financials, industry trends, and market conditions.

3. Lack of diversification: Investing in individual stocks may lead to a lack of diversification, as your investments are concentrated in specific companies or sectors.

- **Bonds:** Bonds are fixed-income securities issued by governments or corporations. They pay interest over a specific period, providing a steady income stream.

Pros:

1. Steady income stream: Bonds pay regular interest over a specific period, providing a predictable income stream.

2. Capital preservation: Bonds are generally considered less risky than stocks, as they offer a fixed return of principal at maturity.

3. Diversification: Bonds can be an effective tool for diversification, as they have different risk profiles than stocks.

Cons:

1. Lower potential for high returns: Bonds typically offer lower returns compared to stocks, especially in periods of low interest rates.

2. Interest rate risk: Bond prices are inversely related to interest rates. If interest rates rise, the value of existing bonds may decrease.

3. Default risk: There is a risk that the issuer of the bond may default on interest or principal payments.

- **Mutual Funds:** Mutual funds pool money from multiple investors to invest in a diversified portfolio of stocks, bonds, or other assets. They offer instant diversification and professional management.

Pros:

1. Diversification: Mutual funds offer instant diversification as they invest in a wide range of assets, spreading risk across different securities or asset classes.

2. Professional management: Mutual funds are managed by professional fund managers who make investment decisions on behalf of the investors.

3. Accessibility: Mutual funds are easily accessible to individual investors, even with smaller amounts of capital.

4. Liquidity: Most mutual funds allow investors to buy or sell shares on any business day.

Cons:

1. Fees: Mutual funds charge fees, such as expense ratios and sales loads, which can impact overall returns.

2. Lack of control: Investing in mutual funds means relinquishing control of individual investment decisions to the fund manager.

3. Potential for underperformance: Not all mutual funds perform well, and some may underperform their benchmarks or similar investment options.

- **Exchange-Traded Funds (ETFs):** ETFs are similar to mutual funds but trade on stock exchanges like individual stocks. They provide diversification and are often more cost-effective.

Practical Tip: Start investing with small amounts and consider low-cost index funds or

ETFs, which provide broad market exposure and are suitable for beginners.

Case Study: Ethan, a determined young investor, recognizes the potential of the stock market to grow his savings. With careful planning and a long-term perspective, he sets out on his investment journey. Let's delve into Ethan's investment success story:

Thorough Research: Ethan understands the importance of conducting thorough research before making investment decisions. He spends time analyzing companies, studying their financial health, evaluating industry trends, and assessing their long-term growth potential. By arming himself with knowledge, Ethan makes informed investment choices.

Diversified Portfolio: Recognizing the value of diversification, Ethan ensures that his investment portfolio is well-balanced. Rather than putting all his eggs in one basket, he spreads his investments across different sectors and companies. This diversification helps mitigate risk by reducing the impact of any individual investment's performance on his overall portfolio.

Long-Term Investment Approach: Ethan adopts a long-term investment approach, understanding that the stock market can experience short-term fluctuations. Instead of being swayed by market noise or succumbing to impulsive trading, he remains focused on his investment goals and stays invested for the long haul. This patient approach allows him to ride out market volatility and benefit from potential long-term growth.

Significant Returns: Ethan's commitment to research, diversification, and a long-term approach pays off. Over time, his investments generate significant returns, surpassing his initial expectations. The growth in his investment portfolio not only provides him with financial security but also presents an opportunity to fund his college education.

Funding College Education: Thanks to the success of his investments, Ethan can fulfill his dream of pursuing a college education. The returns from his investment portfolio offer him the necessary financial resources to cover tuition fees, books, and other educational expenses. Ethan's investment success not only enhances his academic journey but also sets a solid foundation for his future financial well-being.

Ethan's story highlights the power of informed decision-making, diversification, and a long-term investment perspective. By following his footsteps and applying similar strategies, young investors can set themselves on a path towards financial growth and accomplishment. However, it's important to remember that investing involves risks, and individual results may vary. Conducting thorough research, seeking professional advice, and staying committed to long-term goals are key factors in achieving investment success.

Long-Term Saving Strategies: Long-term saving strategies are crucial for building wealth and securing your financial future. Here are some key strategies to consider:

1. **Individual Retirement Accounts (IRAs):** IRAs are powerful tools for retirement savings. They offer tax

advantages that can help your savings grow more efficiently over time. There are two main types of IRAs to consider:

- **Traditional IRAs:** With a traditional IRA, your contributions may be tax-deductible, which can lower your current taxable income. The earnings on your investments grow tax-deferred until you withdraw the funds in retirement, at which point they are subject to taxes.

- **Roth IRAs:** Roth IRAs are funded with after-tax contributions, meaning you don't get an immediate tax deduction. However, the growth and withdrawals in retirement are generally tax-free. This can provide significant advantages, especially if you expect to be in a higher tax bracket during retirement.

2. **Employer-Sponsored Retirement Plans:** Many employers offer retirement plans such as 401(k)s or

403(b)s. These plans allow you to contribute a portion of your salary towards retirement savings, often with the added benefit of employer matching contributions. Take full advantage of these plans by contributing at least enough to receive the maximum matching contribution. Employer-sponsored plans provide a tax-advantaged way to save for retirement and can significantly boost your long-term savings.

3. **Dollar-Cost Averaging:** Dollar-cost averaging is a strategy that involves investing a fixed amount of money at regular intervals, regardless of market conditions. By investing consistently over time, you buy more shares when prices are low and fewer shares when prices are high. This approach helps smooth out the impact of market volatility and reduces the risk of making poorly timed investment decisions. It allows you to take advantage of market fluctuations and

potentially achieve a lower average cost per share over the long term.

These long-term saving strategies provide a solid foundation for building wealth and achieving financial security. By utilizing tax-advantaged retirement accounts, taking advantage of employer-sponsored plans, and employing dollar-cost averaging, you can make significant progress towards your retirement goals. Remember, it's essential to start saving early and stay disciplined in your contributions to maximize the potential benefits of these strategies. Consider consulting with a financial advisor to tailor these strategies to your specific needs and goals.

Interactive Exercise: Plan for Retirement Use an online retirement calculator to estimate how much you need to save for retirement. Determine how much you should contribute monthly or annually to reach your retirement savings goal. Consider the power of compounding and the potential impact of starting early.

Chapter 3: Banking and Financial Services

Banks are essential institutions that play a vital role in managing personal finances and providing a wide range of financial services. Let's explore some of the key offerings and benefits provided by banks:

1. **Deposit Accounts:** Banks offer a variety of deposit accounts to cater to different needs. These include:

   - **Checking Accounts:** Checking accounts are designed for everyday transactions, such as paying bills, making purchases, and withdrawing cash. They often come with features like debit cards, online banking, and mobile banking apps for convenient access to funds.

   - **Savings Accounts:** Savings accounts are intended for storing money and earning interest. They provide a safe place to keep your funds while allowing them to grow over time. Many banks offer competitive interest rates on savings accounts, helping your money work for you.

2. **Loans and Credit:** Banks are known for providing loans and credit facilities to help individuals achieve their financial goals. Some common types of loans offered by banks include:

    *   **Student Loans:** Banks offer student loans to assist with funding higher education expenses. These loans typically have competitive interest rates and flexible repayment options.

    *   **Car Loans:** If you're planning to purchase a car, banks provide auto loans that allow you to finance the purchase over a specific period. These loans make it easier to afford a vehicle by spreading the cost over time.

- **Mortgages:** Banks offer mortgages, which are long-term loans used to finance the purchase of a home. With favorable interest rates and repayment terms, mortgages make homeownership more accessible for many individuals.

- **Credit Cards:** Banks issue credit cards that enable convenient payment options. Credit cards allow you to make purchases and pay them off over time, providing flexibility and a line of credit when needed.

3. **Financial Management Tools:** Banks provide customers with a range of tools and services to assist in managing their finances effectively. These tools include:

- **Online and Mobile Banking:** Banks offer secure online and mobile banking platforms, allowing customers to access their accounts, check balances, transfer funds, and make payments from the convenience of their devices.

- **Budgeting Tools:** Many banks provide budgeting tools and resources to help customers track their spending, set financial goals, and manage their money effectively. These tools offer insights into spending patterns and provide guidance for better financial management.

- **Account Management Features:** Banks offer features like automated bill payments, direct deposit, and account alerts to simplify financial management. These features ensure that bills are paid on time, deposits are received efficiently, and customers stay informed about their account activity.

Banks serve as valuable financial partners, offering a wide range of services to meet the diverse needs of individuals. Whether you need a safe place to store your money, financial assistance for significant purchases, or tools to manage your finances, banks are there to support your financial journey.

Interactive Exercise: Research Local Banks
Take some time to research local banks and

compare their offerings. Consider factors like fees, interest rates, online banking capabilities, and customer reviews. Make a list of pros and cons for each bank.

Types of Bank Accounts

Understanding the different types of bank accounts will help you make informed decisions about where to keep your money. Here are the most common types:

- **Checking Accounts:** These accounts allow for frequent transactions, such as paying bills and making purchases using checks or debit cards. They usually offer low to no interest.

- **Savings Accounts:** Savings accounts are designed to help you save money and earn interest on your deposits. They have limited withdrawal options to encourage saving.

- **Certificates of Deposit (CDs):** CDs are time deposits with fixed terms and interest rates. They offer higher interest rates compared to regular savings accounts, but you must commit to leaving the money untouched for a specific period.

- **Money Market Accounts:** Money market accounts are a hybrid between savings and checking accounts. They typically offer higher interest rates than regular savings accounts but have higher minimum balance requirements.

Practical Tip: Assess your financial goals and determine which account types align with your needs. Consider opening multiple accounts to separate funds for different purposes.

Case Study: Lisa, a young and financially savvy individual, understands the importance of effectively managing her money. She develops a strategic approach by utilizing different types of bank accounts to optimize her financial management. Let's explore how Lisa's account strategy helps her achieve her financial goals:

1. *Checking Account: Lisa opens a checking account, which serves as her primary account for day-to-day transactions. This account provides her*

with easy access to her funds and offers features like a debit card, online banking, and mobile banking apps. Lisa uses her checking account to conveniently pay bills, make purchases, and withdraw cash as needed. By keeping her spending money separate from her long-term savings, Lisa ensures that her daily financial needs are met while maintaining clear visibility of her transactional activities.

2. *Savings Account: Lisa recognizes the importance of building an emergency fund for unexpected expenses. To achieve this, she opens a savings account. This account provides a safe place for Lisa to store her money while earning interest on her savings. By regularly depositing a portion of her income into her savings account, Lisa systematically grows her emergency fund. This financial cushion provides her with peace of mind, knowing that she is prepared for unexpected financial challenges that may arise.*

3. *Certificate of Deposit (CD): Lisa also considers long-term savings as a part of her financial strategy. She decides to open a Certificate of Deposit (CD), which offers higher interest rates compared to regular savings accounts. Lisa understands that a CD requires her to deposit a specific amount of money for a fixed period. In return, she receives a guaranteed interest rate. Lisa carefully selects a CD term that aligns with her long-term savings goals and risk tolerance. By investing in a CD, Lisa ensures that her savings grow steadily over time, providing her with a reliable source of future income.*

Through her thoughtful account strategy, Lisa optimizes her financial management. She segregates her funds by utilizing a checking account for everyday expenses, a savings account for emergency funds, and a CD for long-term savings. This approach allows Lisa to effectively allocate her money, earn interest on her savings, and have access to funds tailored to specific financial needs. By employing these different account types, Lisa demonstrates her commitment to financial responsibility and sets herself up for a secure and prosperous financial future.

Using Financial Services: Financial services go beyond basic banking and encompass various tools and resources to support your financial well-being. Here are some common financial services to explore:

- **Online and Mobile Banking:** Take advantage of online and mobile banking platforms to conveniently manage your accounts, track expenses, and set financial goals.

- **ATM Services:** Utilize ATMs to withdraw cash, deposit checks, and check your account balances. Be mindful of ATM fees and use your bank's network to avoid additional charges.

- **Money Transfer Services:** If you need to send money to family or friends, explore reliable money transfer services that offer secure and cost-effective options.

Practical Tip: Regularly review your bank statements and transaction history to detect any errors or unauthorized charges. Report any discrepancies to your bank immediately.

Interactive Exercise: Log in to your online banking platform and explore the various features and tools available. Set up alerts for account activity, create a budgeting plan, and practice transferring money between accounts.

Understanding Credit and Loans

Credit and loans can be valuable financial tools, but it's essential to understand how they work and use them responsibly. Here's an overview:

- **Credit Scores:** Your credit score reflects your creditworthiness and affects your ability to borrow money. Maintain a good credit score by paying bills on time, keeping credit card balances low, and managing debt responsibly.

- **Credit Cards:** Credit cards offer convenience and a line of credit. Use them wisely, pay off the balance in full each month, and avoid excessive debt.

- **Student Loans:** If you're considering higher education, research and compare student loan options. Borrow only what you need, understand the terms and repayment options, and explore scholarships and grants first.

Practical Tip: Regularly review your credit report to ensure accuracy and address any errors promptly. Aim to build a positive credit history by responsibly managing credit.

Case Study: Mark, a financially responsible individual, understands the importance of maintaining a good credit history. He decides to obtain a credit card and uses it wisely, showcasing his responsible credit behavior. Let's delve into how Mark's responsible credit use leads to numerous benefits:

1. *Paying the Balance in Full: Mark understands that carrying a balance on his credit card can lead to accumulating interest charges. To avoid unnecessary debt, Mark diligently pays the balance*

in full each month. By doing so, he avoids interest fees and ensures that he only spends what he can afford. This responsible payment behavior demonstrates his financial discipline and helps him maintain control over his credit card usage.

2. *Avoiding Unnecessary Debt: Mark uses his credit card for planned purchases and emergencies, rather than relying on it for impulsive or unnecessary expenses. He recognizes that using credit responsibly means spending within his means and not exceeding his budget. By avoiding unnecessary debt, Mark maintains a healthy financial outlook and prevents himself from falling into a cycle of unmanageable debt.*

3. *Maintaining a Good Credit Score: Mark understands that his credit score is an essential factor in financial decision-making. By consistently paying his credit card bill on time and in full, Mark establishes a positive payment history, which contributes to a strong credit*

score. He also keeps his credit utilization low by not maxing out his credit limit. Mark's responsible credit behavior and good credit score open doors to numerous opportunities.

4. *Eligibility for Better Loan Terms: Mark's responsible credit use positions him as a desirable borrower in the eyes of lenders. When he applies for loans, such as auto loans or mortgages, his excellent credit history and high credit score make him eligible for better loan terms. Mark can secure lower interest rates, more favorable repayment terms, and potentially save a significant amount of money over time.*

5. *Enjoying Benefits of a Strong Credit History: As Mark continues to use his credit card responsibly, his credit history strengthens. This opens up opportunities to access additional credit, such as higher credit limits or other credit products. He may also be eligible for rewards programs, cashback offers, or*

other credit card perks that come with responsible credit use.

By employing responsible credit card habits, Mark showcases his financial maturity and establishes a strong foundation for his credit history. His diligent payment practices and avoidance of unnecessary debt contribute to a healthy financial profile. As a result, Mark enjoys the benefits of better loan terms, improved financial opportunities, and the peace of mind that comes with responsible credit use.

Chapter 4: Earning and Managing Income

As you enter the workforce or consider entrepreneurial opportunities, it's important to develop a solid understanding of how to maximize your earning potential and effectively manage your income. By learning about part-time jobs, entrepreneurship, paycheck management, networking, salary negotiation, and career planning, you will be better equipped to make informed decisions and build a successful financial future. Let's dive into the world of earning and managing income.

In addition to saving and investing, part-time jobs and entrepreneurship provide valuable avenues for young individuals to earn income and develop essential skills. Let's delve into the details of these opportunities and what you need to know about them:

1. **Part-Time Jobs:** Part-time jobs offer a range of benefits beyond just earning

money. They provide an opportunity to gain work experience, develop valuable skills, and explore potential career paths. Here are some key considerations when exploring part-time job opportunities:

- **Aligning with Interests and Schedule:** Look for part-time job options that align with your interests, talents, and career aspirations. This will make your work more fulfilling and enjoyable. Additionally, consider the flexibility of the job and how it fits into your schedule, especially if you have other commitments such as school or extracurricular activities.

- **Transferable Skills:** Part-time jobs can help you develop transferable skills that will be valuable in various aspects of your life. These skills can include communication, teamwork, problem-solving, customer service, and time management. Emphasize these skills on your resume and during job interviews to showcase your potential to future employers.

- **Pay and Compensation:** While pay is an important factor to consider, it's not the sole determining factor. Look beyond just the hourly wage and consider other benefits such as employee discounts, opportunities for advancement, or skill-building programs that the job may offer.

2. **Entrepreneurship:** If you have an entrepreneurial spirit and are willing to take on the challenges of starting your own business, entrepreneurship can be an exciting and rewarding path to explore. Here are some key steps to get started:

- **Market Research:** Before starting a business, thoroughly research your target market. Identify the needs, preferences, and pain points of your potential customers. This will help you tailor your product or service to meet their demands effectively.

- **Business Plan:** Develop a well-thought-out business plan that outlines your vision, goals, target audience, marketing strategies, financial projections, and operational details. A comprehensive business plan will guide you through the various stages of setting up and running your business.

- **Financial Considerations:** Starting a business requires initial investment and ongoing financial management. Assess your financial situation and determine how much capital you'll need to launch your venture. Explore funding options such as personal savings, loans, or grants.

- **Persistence and Adaptability:** Entrepreneurship often involves facing challenges and setbacks. Maintain a mindset of persistence and adaptability as you navigate obstacles and learn from your experiences. Embrace innovation and be open to adjusting your business strategies based on market feedback.

Both part-time jobs and entrepreneurship offer unique opportunities for income generation, skill development, and personal growth. Whether you choose to work for someone else or embark on your entrepreneurial journey, these experiences can shape your financial future and provide you with valuable insights and abilities that extend beyond just financial gains.

Practical Tip: Before committing to a part-time job or entrepreneurship, consider your availability, long-term goals, and the potential impact on your studies or other commitments.

Understanding Paychecks and Taxes

To effectively manage your income, it is crucial to have a solid understanding of how paychecks and taxes work. Let's delve into the key points you need to consider:

1. **Gross vs. Net Income:** When looking at your paycheck, it is important to distinguish between gross income and net income. Gross income refers to the total amount you earn before any deductions, such as taxes or contributions. Net income, on the other hand, is the amount you receive after these deductions. It is the actual income that you can use for your expenses and savings.

2. **Withholdings and Deductions:** Paycheck deductions are amounts withheld from your gross income to cover various expenses and obligations. It is essential to familiarize yourself with common paycheck deductions, including:

    *   **Federal and State Taxes:** The government levies income taxes at both the federal and state levels. The specific amount deducted depends on factors such as your

income level and the tax brackets applicable in your jurisdiction.

- **Social Security and Medicare Contributions:** Paycheck deductions also include contributions to Social Security and Medicare. These contributions are made to fund these programs, which provide benefits and medical coverage during retirement and certain health conditions.

It is important to review your paycheck regularly to ensure the accuracy of these deductions. Mistakes or discrepancies can result in either overpaying or underpaying your taxes and other obligations.

3. **Paycheck Frequency:** Paychecks can be issued on a weekly, bi-weekly, or monthly basis, depending on your employer's pay schedule. Understanding your paycheck frequency is crucial for budgeting and managing your expenses. It helps you align your income with your financial obligations, such as bills, rent, and

other monthly expenses. Consider the timing of your paychecks when creating a budget to ensure that you allocate your income effectively throughout the month.

By comprehending the distinction between gross and net income, being aware of common paycheck deductions, and understanding your paycheck frequency, you can effectively manage your income. This knowledge allows you to create realistic budgets, plan for expenses, and make informed financial decisions. Keep in mind that tax laws and regulations may vary based on your location, so it's advisable to consult with a tax professional or utilize reliable resources to stay up to date with the specific tax obligations in your area.

Interactive Exercise: Calculate Your Net Income Use an online paycheck calculator or a sample paycheck to calculate your net income. Consider different scenarios by adjusting deductions and withholdings. Determine the impact on your take-home pay.

Building a Professional Network

A strong professional network is a valuable asset that can open doors to new opportunities, help you stay updated on industry trends, and provide valuable support throughout your career journey. Here are some tips to help you build and cultivate a robust professional network:

1. **Attend Networking Events:** Actively participate in industry-specific events, career fairs, and workshops. These events provide excellent opportunities to meet professionals in your field of interest, expand your knowledge, and forge connections. Engage in meaningful conversations, exchange contact information, and follow up with individuals you meet to foster lasting connections.

2. **Utilize Social Media:** In today's digital age, social media platforms offer powerful tools for professional networking. Create a strong online presence, particularly on platforms like LinkedIn, which is designed for

professional networking. Optimize your profile, highlight your skills and experiences, and connect with colleagues, peers, and industry professionals. Join relevant groups, participate in discussions, and share valuable insights to demonstrate your expertise and engage with others in your field.

3. **Seek Mentorship:** Finding mentors who have expertise and experience in your desired field can be immensely beneficial for your career growth. Seek out individuals who can offer guidance, share insights, and provide support as you navigate your professional journey. Look for mentors within your organization, professional associations, or through networking events. Establish meaningful relationships with mentors by actively seeking their advice, sharing your goals and aspirations, and demonstrating your commitment to learning and growth.

4. **Offer Value to Others:** Networking is a two-way street. To build meaningful connections, it is important to offer value to others in your network. Share relevant articles, resources, or insights that may benefit your connections. Offer your assistance or expertise whenever possible. By providing value to others, you establish yourself as a trusted and valuable member of your professional network.

5. **Follow Up and Stay Connected:** After attending networking events or engaging with professionals, remember to follow up and maintain connections. Send personalized follow-up emails or LinkedIn messages to express your gratitude for the conversation and express your interest in staying connected. Regularly reach out to your network, whether through occasional messages, attending industry-related webinars, or meeting for coffee. Consistent communication helps to strengthen relationships and keep you

top   of   mind   for   potential
opportunities.

Remember, building a strong professional
network takes time and effort. It is an ongoing
process that requires consistent engagement
and   nurturing.   By   actively   attending
networking events, utilizing social media
platforms, seeking mentorship, offering value
to others, and staying connected, you can
establish a robust professional network that
supports your career growth and opens doors
to exciting opportunities.

Practical Tip: Prepare an elevator pitch that
succinctly describes your skills, interests, and
career goals. This will help you make a strong
impression when networking.

Negotiating Salary and Benefits

Negotiating salary and benefits is a crucial skill
to develop as you progress in your career. It
allows you to advocate for your worth and
secure a compensation package that aligns with
your skills, experience, and contributions. Here
are some essential tips to consider when
engaging in salary negotiations:

1. **Research Market Salaries:** Before entering into negotiations, it's important to have a solid understanding of the market value for positions similar to the one you are applying for. Research salary ranges and industry standards to ensure that your expectations are realistic and aligned with current market trends. This information will serve as a valuable reference point during the negotiation process.

2. **Highlight Your Value:** During negotiations, it's essential to confidently communicate the value you bring to the organization. Emphasize your skills, qualifications, achievements, and any unique experiences that set you apart from other candidates. Clearly articulate how your contributions can positively impact the company's goals and bottom line. By effectively highlighting your value, you can strengthen your position and make a compelling case for a higher salary or better benefits.

3. **Consider Total Compensation:** Salary is just one aspect of your overall compensation package. When negotiating, it's important to evaluate and consider other benefits that can significantly impact your job satisfaction and financial well-being. Factors such as healthcare benefits, retirement plans, paid vacation time, flexible work arrangements, and professional development opportunities should be taken into account. Assess the value of these benefits and weigh them against the salary being offered. Sometimes, a lower salary with exceptional benefits can be more advantageous in the long run.

4. **Be Prepared to Negotiate:** Enter salary negotiations with a clear plan and a desired outcome in mind. Set a realistic salary range based on your research and personal circumstances. Consider any factors that may warrant a higher salary, such as advanced qualifications, specialized skills, or relevant industry

experience. Anticipate potential counteroffers or objections from the employer and be prepared to address them confidently and professionally. Practice your negotiation skills beforehand to ensure you convey your points effectively.

5. **Remain Professional and Collaborative:** Remember that salary negotiations are not adversarial but rather a collaborative effort to find a mutually beneficial agreement. Maintain a professional and respectful demeanor throughout the process. Listen actively to the employer's perspective and be open to constructive dialogue. Seek common ground and propose creative solutions that address both your needs and the employer's budget constraints. Finding a win-win outcome is the ideal result of successful negotiations.

6. **Know Your Bottom Line:** While it's important to be flexible during negotiations, it's also crucial to have a

clear understanding of your minimum acceptable salary and benefits. Determine your bottom line in advance, considering your financial obligations, living expenses, and long-term financial goals. If an offer falls significantly below your minimum requirements, be prepared to graciously decline and continue your job search.

Negotiation is a skill that improves with practice. The more you engage in salary negotiations, the more confident and effective you will become. By conducting thorough research, highlighting your value, considering total compensation, being prepared, maintaining professionalism, and knowing your bottom line, you can maximize your chances of securing a fair and rewarding compensation package that recognizes your contributions and supports your career growth.

Interactive Exercise: Role-Play Salary Negotiations Pair up with a friend or classmate and role-play a salary negotiation scenario. Take turns being the employer and

the employee. Practice effective communication, persuasion, and negotiation techniques.

Career Planning and Advancement

Strategic career planning and continuous learning are essential for long-term success in today's dynamic and competitive job market. By implementing effective strategies, you can proactively shape your career trajectory and stay ahead of the curve.

Setting clear goals is the first step in strategic career planning. Take the time to reflect on your passions, interests, and aspirations. Define specific career goals and create a roadmap to achieve them. Break down your long-term goals into manageable short-term milestones, allowing you to track your progress and make necessary adjustments along the way. Clear goals provide direction and motivation, helping you stay focused on your desired career path.

Investing in education and skills development is crucial for staying relevant and competitive in your field. Continuously seek opportunities to enhance your knowledge and expertise. This may involve pursuing formal education such as degree programs or specialized certifications. Additionally, consider attending workshops, seminars, and conferences to stay up to date with the latest industry trends and best practices. Take advantage of online learning platforms that offer a wide range of courses and resources tailored to your professional development needs. By constantly expanding your skills and knowledge, you position yourself as a valuable asset to employers and increase your career advancement opportunities.

Seeking growth opportunities within your current organization or industry is another important strategy for career advancement. Take on challenging assignments or projects that allow you to develop new skills and showcase your capabilities. Actively seek feedback from supervisors, mentors, or colleagues to identify areas for improvement and growth. Embrace opportunities for promotions or lateral moves that align with your long-term goals. Networking and building relationships within your industry can also open doors to new opportunities and career growth.

It's important to note that career planning and continuous learning require adaptability and flexibility. The job market and industry landscapes are constantly evolving, so it's essential to stay agile and embrace change. Regularly reassess your goals, update your skills, and stay informed about emerging trends in your field. Be open to new possibilities and seize opportunities for professional growth and development.

By implementing strategic career planning and committing to continuous learning, you can position yourself for long-term success and fulfillment in your chosen career. Remember to set clear goals, invest in education and skills, and actively seek growth opportunities. With dedication and perseverance, you can navigate your career path with confidence and achieve your professional aspirations.

Practical Tip: Build a professional development fund as part of your budget. Allocate a portion of your income toward

acquiring new skills and attending relevant conferences or workshops.

Case Study: Sandra, a determined and ambitious young professional, embarks on a journey of career advancement by setting clear goals and investing in her education. Through her proactive efforts, she paves the way for success and ultimately achieves remarkable growth within her chosen field. Here are the key steps she takes on her path to career advancement:

1. *Defining Clear Career Goals: Sandra starts by identifying her career aspirations and setting clear goals. She takes the time to reflect on her passions, strengths, and long-term ambitions. By defining her career trajectory, she gains a sense of direction and purpose, which serves as a guiding force throughout her journey.*

2. *Investing in Education: Recognizing the value of continuous learning, Sandra takes steps to enhance her knowledge and skills. She identifies relevant*

certifications or courses that can provide her with specialized expertise in her field. By dedicating time and effort to her education, she not only expands her knowledge base but also demonstrates her commitment to professional growth and development.

3. *Attending Industry Conferences: Sandra actively seeks opportunities to attend industry conferences and networking events. These events allow her to stay updated on the latest trends, connect with like-minded professionals, and broaden her professional network. By immersing herself in her industry's community, Sandra gains valuable insights and exposure to new ideas and opportunities.*

4. *Seeking Growth Opportunities: Within her current organization, Sandra proactively seeks out growth opportunities. She takes on challenging projects, volunteers for cross-functional teams, and seeks mentorship from experienced colleagues. By actively*

participating in diverse projects and initiatives, Sandra expands her skill set, showcases her capabilities, and demonstrates her willingness to contribute beyond her current role.

5. *Demonstrating Dedication and Continuous Learning: Sandra's dedication to personal and professional growth shines through her actions. She stays abreast of industry news, reads relevant books and articles, and consistently seeks opportunities for self-improvement. By demonstrating a growth mindset and a commitment to continuous learning, Sandra sets herself apart and establishes herself as a valuable asset within her organization.*

6. *Achieving Promotion and Increased Earning Potential: Sandra's hard work, dedication, and continuous learning pay off as she earns a well-deserved promotion within her company. Her commitment to self-improvement and her track record of success make her an ideal candidate for advancement. With*

her promotion comes increased responsibilities, recognition, and the potential for higher earning potential, setting her on a trajectory of success in her career.

Sandra's journey serves as an inspiration for young professionals seeking career advancement. By setting clear goals, investing in education, attending industry events, seeking growth opportunities, demonstrating dedication, and embracing continuous learning, Sandra not only achieves her desired career progression but also establishes herself as a valued and respected professional in her field. Her success is a testament to the power of perseverance, proactive learning, and seizing opportunities for growth.

Chapter 5: Consumer Skills and Financial Decision Making

As a consumer, it's important to evaluate your needs versus wants, practice comparison shopping, understand advertising tactics, make informed purchase decisions, and be aware of your consumer rights and protections. By developing these skills, you will become a smart and responsible consumer, ensuring that your money is spent wisely. Let's dive into the world of consumer skills and financial decision making.

Evaluating Needs vs. Wants: Understanding the distinction between needs and wants is essential for making informed and responsible spending decisions. Here are some key points to consider:

- **Needs:** Needs are fundamental items or services necessary for your basic survival and well-being. These include essentials like food, water, shelter, clothing, and healthcare. Meeting these needs is crucial for maintaining a decent quality of life and ensuring your health and safety.

- **Wants:** Wants, on the other hand, are desires for non-essential items or services that provide enjoyment, comfort, or convenience. While fulfilling wants can enhance your lifestyle and bring you satisfaction, they are not necessary for your survival or basic well-being.

Recognizing the difference between needs and wants helps you prioritize your spending and allocate your resources more effectively. By focusing on meeting your needs first, you can ensure that you have a solid foundation of essential items before indulging in discretionary wants.

Interactive Exercise: Identify Needs vs. Wants Create a list of items or services you desire. Review each item and determine if it is a need or a want. Discuss with a friend or family member to gain different perspectives.

Comparison Shopping and Research: Comparison shopping is a valuable practice that allows you to make informed decisions and get the best value for your money. Here are some strategies for effective comparison shopping:

- **Research:** Before making a purchase, invest time in researching different brands, models, or service providers. Take advantage of online resources, read customer reviews, and seek out professional opinions. This research helps you gather information and gain insights into the quality, features, and reputation of the products or services you are considering.

- **Consider Quality and Price:** When comparing products or services, consider both their quality and price. Assess the features, durability, and performance of similar options to determine the overall value they offer. It's important to strike a balance between quality and affordability to ensure that you get the most out of your purchase.

- **Look Beyond Price:** While price is an important factor, it's essential to look beyond it when comparing products or services. Consider additional factors such as warranties, customer support, return policies, and any extra benefits offered. Evaluating these aspects helps you make a more comprehensive assessment and choose the option that aligns with your needs and preferences.

By engaging in comparison shopping and thorough research, you empower yourself to make informed decisions and avoid impulsive purchases. This approach allows you to optimize your spending by selecting products or services that meet your requirements while providing the best possible value.

Practical Tip: Use **online resources, review websites, and price comparison tools to streamline your research and find the best deals.**

Case Study: Sam is in the market for a new laptop and understands the importance of making a smart purchase. Rather than impulsively buying the first laptop that catches their eye, Sam takes a systematic approach to ensure they make an informed decision. Here's how Sam goes about their smart purchase:

1. *Thorough Research: Sam begins by conducting thorough research on laptops. They explore different brands, models, and specifications to gain a comprehensive understanding of the available options.*

2. *Brand and Model Comparison: Sam compares various laptop brands and models based on factors like performance, reliability, durability, and customer reviews. They pay attention to key features that align with their specific needs and preferences.*

3. *Customer Reviews: Sam values the opinions and experiences of other customers. They read online reviews and testimonials to gather insights into the real-world performance and satisfaction levels of the laptops they are considering.*

4. *Pricing and Features Analysis: Sam carefully considers the pricing of the*

laptops they are interested in, comparing them against the features and benefits offered. They weigh the value of each option to ensure they are getting the best possible combination of performance and affordability.

By following these steps, Sam successfully finds a high-quality laptop that meets their requirements while also being competitively priced. Their thorough research and comparison shopping help them make an informed decision, ultimately resulting in a smart purchase that provides both satisfaction and value for their investment.

Understanding Advertising and Marketing Tactics

Understanding advertising and marketing tactics is crucial in today's consumer-driven world. It empowers individuals to make informed decisions, resist impulsive purchases, and maintain control over their financial well-being. Here are key points to consider when it comes to understanding advertising and marketing tactics:

1. **Identify Persuasive Techniques:** Advertising techniques are designed to capture your attention and persuade you to buy a product or service. It's important to be aware of common persuasive techniques used in marketing, such as:

   - **Emotional Appeals:** Advertisements often evoke emotions to create a connection between the product and your desires or aspirations. Recognizing emotional manipulation can help you evaluate advertisements critically and make rational decisions.

   - **Celebrity Endorsements:** Brands frequently use celebrities to endorse their products, hoping to leverage their influence and credibility. However, it's essential to evaluate the actual value and relevance of the celebrity endorsement to the product itself.

- **Limited-Time Offers:** Creating a sense of urgency through limited-time offers or deals can influence impulsive buying behavior. Take the time to assess the actual value of the offer and whether it aligns with your needs and budget.

2. **Differentiate Between Needs and Desires:** Advertisements are often designed to create desires for products or services, even if they may not be essential to your well-being. It's crucial to differentiate between genuine needs and desires influenced by advertising:

- **Genuine Needs:** Identify your genuine needs based on practical considerations and personal priorities. These are the necessities required for your daily life, well-being, and long-term goals.

- **Desires Influenced by Advertising:** Be mindful of desires influenced by advertising that may not align with your true needs. Question whether the product or service is genuinely necessary or if it's driven by marketing tactics that play on emotions or societal pressures.

By understanding advertising and marketing tactics, you can develop a critical mindset when encountering advertisements. This awareness enables you to make informed decisions, resist impulsive purchases, and prioritize your spending based on genuine needs and long-term financial goals.

Practical Tip: Practice skepticism when evaluating advertisements. Look beyond flashy promotions and focus on the product's actual value and suitability for your needs.

Interactive Exercise: Select a few advertisements from different mediums (TV, print, online) and critically analyze them. Identify the persuasive techniques used, the target audience, and the intended message. Share your analysis with a group to encourage discussion.

Making Informed Purchase Decisions: Making informed purchase decisions involves considering multiple factors and assessing the value of a product or service. Here's what you should consider:

- **Cost-Benefit Analysis:** Evaluate the value you will derive from a product or service compared to its cost. Consider factors such as quality, durability, functionality, and long-term use.

- **Environmental Impact:** Assess the environmental impact of a product, such as its energy efficiency, recyclability, and sustainability practices of the manufacturer.

- **Ethical Considerations:** Consider the ethical practices of the company, such as fair labor practices, transparency, and social responsibility.

Practical Tip: Create a decision matrix where you weigh different factors and assign them a value to make more informed purchase decisions.

Consumer Rights and Protection: Understanding your consumer rights and protections is essential for ensuring fair and safe transactions. Here's what you need to know:

- **Consumer Rights:** Familiarize yourself with your rights as a consumer, such as the right to safety, the right to information, and the right to complain.

- **Product Warranties:** Understand the terms of product warranties and know your options for repairs, replacements, or refunds.

- **Consumer Protection Agencies:** Be aware of consumer protection agencies that can assist you in resolving disputes or reporting fraudulent activities.

Practical Tip: Keep records of your purchases, including receipts, warranties, and correspondence, to protect yourself in case of any issues.

Chapter 6:
Understanding Debt and Managing Credit

Understanding how debt works, borrowing responsibly, managing student loans, monitoring credit scores and reports, and implementing strategies for debt repayment are essential skills for financial well-being. By developing a comprehensive understanding of debt and credit, you will be able to make informed decisions and maintain a healthy financial life. Let's dive into the world of debt and credit management.

Debt is a financial tool that can provide individuals with the means to fulfill their needs and pursue their goals. Understanding the concept of debt and its implications is essential for making informed financial decisions. Here are some key points to consider:

• **Types of Debt:** Debt comes in various forms, each with its own characteristics and considerations. Common types of debt include credit card debt, student loans, mortgages, and personal loans. Credit card debt involves borrowing money on a revolving line of credit, while student loans are specifically designed to finance education expenses. Mortgages are loans used to purchase real estate, and personal loans are often taken out for various personal purposes. Exploring these different types of debt allows individuals to gain a better understanding of how they work, and the specific terms associated with each.

• **Good Debt vs. Bad Debt:** It's important to distinguish between good debt and bad debt. Good debt refers to borrowing money for investments or assets that have the potential to increase in value or generate income over time. For example, student loans can be considered good debt if they enable individuals to acquire education and skills that enhance their career prospects and earning potential. Similarly, a mortgage can be viewed as good debt if it allows individuals to purchase a home that appreciates in value. On the other hand, bad debt typically involves borrowing for non-essential items or depreciating assets that do not generate long-term value. Accumulating high-interest credit card debt for unnecessary purchases is an example of bad debt that can lead to financial difficulties and hamper overall financial well-being.

Understanding the types of debt and distinguishing between good and bad debt can help individuals make more informed borrowing decisions. It's crucial to carefully consider the purpose, terms, interest rates, and repayment plans associated with each type of debt before taking on any financial obligations. Responsible debt management involves borrowing within one's means, prioritizing debt repayment, and avoiding unnecessary or high-interest debt whenever possible.

Interactive Exercise: Create a decision tree to evaluate whether taking on debt is a wise decision for different scenarios. Consider factors like interest rates, repayment terms, and the potential impact on your financial goals.

Responsible Borrowing

Borrowing money can be a useful tool when managed responsibly, but it's crucial to approach it with careful consideration and a clear plan for repayment. Here are some key points to keep in mind when it comes to responsible borrowing:

• **Evaluate Your Ability to Repay:** Before taking on any debt, it's essential to evaluate your current financial situation and assess your ability to repay the borrowed funds. Consider your income, expenses, and other financial obligations to determine how much you can comfortably allocate towards loan repayments. By borrowing within your means, you can avoid potential financial strain and ensure that you have enough resources to cover your other financial responsibilities.

• **Compare Interest Rates and Terms:** When borrowing money, it's important to shop around and compare different lenders or credit options to find the most favorable interest rates and terms. Lower interest rates can significantly impact the total cost of borrowing and the amount you'll need to repay over time. Take the time to research and consider multiple options to secure the most favorable borrowing terms available to you.

• **Read and Understand the Fine Print:** Before entering into any borrowing agreement, it's crucial to carefully read and understand all the terms and conditions outlined in the loan agreement or credit contract. Pay attention to details such as interest rates, repayment schedules, fees, penalties for late payments or early repayment, and any other important provisions. Understanding the fine print will help you make informed decisions and avoid any surprises or financial pitfalls down the line.

Additionally, it's worth exploring alternatives to borrowing, such as saving up for purchases or considering lower-cost financing options. Responsible borrowing involves a thoughtful assessment of your financial situation, a comparison of borrowing options, and a clear understanding of the terms and obligations associated with the loan. By borrowing responsibly, you can effectively manage your debt, maintain financial stability, and work towards achieving your financial goals.

Practical Tip: Create a budget that incorporates your loan repayments to ensure they align with your overall financial plan.

Case Study: Erika has set her sights on purchasing a new car, but she understands the importance of responsible borrowing. Before diving into a car loan, she takes the following steps to ensure she can manage her debt effectively:

1. *Evaluating Financial Situation: Erika starts by assessing her financial situation. She carefully examines her income, expenses, and savings to determine how much she can comfortably allocate towards a car loan payment each month. By considering her existing financial obligations, she ensures that the loan repayment fits within her budget without straining her finances.*

2. *Comparing Interest Rates: Erika knows that interest rates play a significant role in the total cost of borrowing. She diligently researches different lenders and their interest rates, aiming to secure the most favorable terms. By comparing multiple options, she can select a lender that offers a competitive interest rate,*

minimizing the overall amount she'll need to repay over time.

3. *Reading the Loan Agreement: Understanding the importance of reading the fine print, Erika takes her time to carefully review the loan agreement provided by the lender. She pays close attention to the terms and conditions, including any fees, penalties, or repayment schedules mentioned in the document. By doing so, she ensures that she fully comprehends her obligations and avoids any unexpected surprises or hidden charges.*

4. *Managing Debt Effectively: With her car loan in place, Erika remains committed to managing her debt responsibly. She makes her monthly payments on time, avoiding any late fees or penalties. By staying organized and prioritizing her loan repayment, she maintains a good credit history and continues to strengthen her financial standing.*

Erika's responsible borrowing approach allows her to enjoy the benefits of owning a new car while maintaining financial stability. By carefully evaluating her financial situation, comparing interest rates, and understanding the loan agreement, she sets herself up for successful debt management and financial well-being.

Managing Student Loans

Student loans are a significant aspect of many college students' financial lives and managing them effectively is crucial. Here are key points to consider when dealing with student loans:

1. **Know Your Options:** It's essential to familiarize yourself with the different types of student loans available. Federal loans, such as Direct Subsidized Loans and Direct Unsubsidized Loans, have specific terms, interest rates, and repayment options. Private loans, on the other hand, are provided by banks or financial institutions and may have different terms and conditions. Understanding the differences between

these options will help you make informed decisions about your borrowing.

2. **Explore Loan Repayment Plans:** When it comes to repaying your student loans, there are various repayment plans to consider. Standard repayment plans typically involve fixed monthly payments over a specific period. Income-driven repayment plans, on the other hand, adjust your monthly payments based on your income and family size, making them more manageable in times of financial uncertainty. Additionally, there are loan forgiveness programs available for those who meet specific eligibility criteria. Research and evaluate these different repayment options to determine which one aligns best with your financial situation and long-term goals.

3. **Make Timely Payments:** It's crucial to prioritize making your student loan payments on time. Late payments can

result in late fees and penalties, negatively impacting your credit score. Setting up automatic payments or reminders can help you stay on track and avoid missing any payments. If you're facing financial difficulties, reach out to your loan servicer to explore options such as deferment, forbearance, or income-driven repayment plans that can provide temporary relief while you get back on your feet.

4. **Communicate with Your Loan Servicer:** If you have any questions or concerns about your student loans, don't hesitate to reach out to your loan servicer. They are there to assist you and can provide guidance on various aspects, such as repayment options, loan consolidation, or eligibility for loan forgiveness programs. Keeping an open line of communication with your loan servicer will ensure you stay informed and receive the support you need.

By understanding your options, exploring repayment plans, and making timely payments, you can effectively manage your student loans and pave the way for a strong financial future. Remember to stay informed about your loans and seek assistance when needed to navigate the complexities of student loan repayment.

Interactive Exercise: Use an online student loan repayment calculator to estimate different repayment scenarios. Explore how adjusting payment amounts, repayment terms, or interest rates can impact your overall loan repayment.

Credit Scores and Reports

Understanding credit scores and reports is crucial for managing credit effectively and accessing financial opportunities. Here are key points to consider:

1. **Credit Scores:** Credit scores are numerical representations of your creditworthiness. They reflect your credit history and indicate the likelihood of you repaying borrowed money. It's essential to learn how credit

scores are calculated and the factors that influence them. Common credit scoring models, such as FICO or VantageScore, consider factors such as your payment history, credit utilization (the amount of credit used compared to your credit limit), length of credit history, types of credit accounts, and recent credit inquiries. Understanding these factors will help you make informed decisions to improve your credit score.

2. **Credit Reports:** Your credit report is a detailed record of your credit history compiled by credit reporting agencies. It includes information about your credit accounts, payment history, credit limits, balances, and any negative information such as late payments or accounts in collections. It's important to review your credit report regularly to ensure the accuracy of the information. By checking your report, you can identify any errors or discrepancies that could potentially impact your credit score. You are entitled to a free

credit report from each of the major credit reporting agencies (Equifax, Experian, and TransUnion) once a year through AnnualCreditReport.com.

3. **Building and Maintaining Good Credit:** Building and maintaining good credit is crucial for accessing favorable loan terms, lower interest rates, and other financial opportunities. To build good credit, make timely payments on all your credit accounts, including loans, credit cards, and utility bills. Keeping your credit card balances low compared to your credit limits (aim for a utilization ratio below 30%) can also positively impact your credit score. Additionally, it's important to avoid excessive debt and only apply for new credit when necessary. Responsible credit behavior over time will help establish a solid credit history and improve your creditworthiness.

4. **Monitoring and Managing Credit:** Regularly monitoring your credit activity is important to stay on top of

your financial health. You can utilize credit monitoring services or apps that provide updates on changes to your credit score and alert you of any suspicious activity. Being proactive in managing your credit allows you to address any issues promptly and protect yourself against identity theft or fraudulent accounts.

Practical Tip: Monitor your credit score and set up alerts or reminders to stay on top of your credit health.

Case Study: John is determined to build and maintain good credit, and he takes proactive steps to achieve this goal. He understands the importance of responsible credit management and implements key strategies.

First and foremost, John prioritizes making timely payments on all his bills, including credit card bills, loans, and other financial obligations. By consistently paying his bills on time, he establishes a positive payment history, which is a crucial factor in determining creditworthiness. This responsible behavior demonstrates to lenders that John is reliable and trustworthy.

Additionally, John understands the significance of keeping his credit card balances low. He avoids maxing out his credit cards and aims to utilize only a small portion of his available credit. By maintaining a low credit utilization ratio, typically below 30%, John showcases his ability to manage credit responsibly. This practice demonstrates to potential lenders that he is not overly reliant on credit and can effectively manage his financial obligations.

John also recognizes the importance of regularly checking his credit report for any errors or discrepancies. He understands that inaccuracies on his credit report can negatively impact his credit score. By reviewing his credit report on a periodic basis, John can promptly identify and address any errors or suspicious activities. This proactive approach ensures that his credit report accurately reflects his financial history and minimizes the risk of potential negative consequences.

As a result of John's diligent efforts in managing his credit, he achieves a favorable credit standing. When applying for his first car loan, John's responsible credit management pays off.

Lenders recognize his positive payment history, low credit utilization, and overall responsible credit behavior. This leads to John being offered a favorable interest rate on his car loan, saving him money in the long run.

John's credit building journey serves as a testament to the importance of responsible credit management. By consistently paying bills on time, keeping credit card balances low, and regularly monitoring his credit report, John successfully establishes and maintains good credit. This not only benefits him in qualifying for loans and favorable interest rates but also provides him with a solid foundation for future financial endeavors.

Strategies for Debt Repayment

Effectively managing and repaying debt is a crucial aspect of maintaining financial well-being. By implementing strategic approaches, individuals can tackle their debts in a structured and efficient manner. Here are some key strategies to consider:

1. **Debt Snowball Method:** This method involves prioritizing debts based on

their balances. Start by identifying the debt with the smallest balance and focus on repaying it aggressively while making minimum payments on other debts. Once the smallest debt is paid off, move on to the next one with the next smallest balance. The debt snowball method provides a psychological boost as each debt is successfully eliminated, creating momentum and motivation to continue the debt repayment journey.

2. **Debt Avalanche Method:** With the debt avalanche method, debts are prioritized based on their interest rates. Begin by identifying the debt with the highest interest rate and allocate extra funds towards paying it off while making minimum payments on other debts. Once the debt with the highest interest rate is cleared, move on to the next debt with the next highest interest rate. This approach can save money on interest payments in the long run.

3. **Debt Consolidation:** Debt consolidation involves combining multiple debts into a single loan with more favorable terms. This can be done by obtaining a consolidation loan or transferring balances to a low-interest credit card. Debt consolidation simplifies the repayment process by consolidating multiple payments into one, potentially reducing the overall interest paid and making it easier to manage debts. However, it's important to carefully evaluate the terms and fees associated with consolidation options to ensure it is a cost-effective solution.

In addition to these strategies, it's essential to adopt good financial habits to effectively manage and repay debt. Create a budget to track income and expenses, allowing for better allocation of funds towards debt repayment. Minimize unnecessary expenses and prioritize debt payments within your budget. Consider seeking professional advice from financial counselors or credit counseling services if you need assistance in developing a debt repayment plan.

Interactive Exercise: Create a debt repayment plan by listing all your debts, including balances, interest rates, and minimum payments. Decide on a strategy (debt snowball or debt avalanche) and determine how much extra you can allocate toward debt repayment each month. Visualize your progress using a debt repayment tracker.

Chapter 7: Planning for the Future

Introduction: Welcome to Chapter 7 of Finance for Youth! In this chapter, we will explore the importance of planning for the future and building a solid financial foundation. By setting financial goals, saving for education, exploring career paths, understanding retirement planning, and building wealth, you will pave the way for a financially secure future. Let's dive into the world of planning for the future.

Setting Financial Goals for the Future: Setting financial goals is a fundamental aspect of achieving financial success. By establishing clear objectives, individuals can create a roadmap for their financial journey. Here's a closer look at what you need to know when setting financial goals:

1. **Short-Term and Long-Term Goals:** Differentiating between short-term and long-term goals is essential. Short-term goals typically have a timeframe of less

than one year and often involve smaller-scale objectives, such as saving for a vacation, paying off a credit card debt, or building an emergency fund. Long-term goals, on the other hand, have a timeframe of more than one year and often involve more significant milestones, such as buying a car, owning a home, or saving for retirement. Distinguishing between these two types of goals allows for better planning and resource allocation.

2. **SMART Goals:** When setting financial goals, it's important to make them SMART—Specific, Measurable, Achievable, Relevant, and Time-bound. By following this framework, you can create goals that are well-defined and actionable. Here's what each component of SMART goals entails:

   - **Specific:** Clearly define your goal with as much detail as possible. Instead of stating "save money," specify the amount you want to save and the purpose of the savings.

- **Measurable:** Set goals that can be measured objectively. Use numbers or quantifiable metrics to track your progress. For example, instead of saying "reduce debt," specify the amount of debt you want to pay off.

- **Achievable:** Ensure your goals are realistic and attainable within your current financial situation. Consider factors such as your income, expenses, and time commitments when setting goals.

- **Relevant:** Align your goals with your broader financial aspirations and values. Ensure they are meaningful to you and contribute to your overall financial well-being.

- **Time-bound:** Establish a timeframe for achieving your goals. This adds a sense of urgency and helps you stay accountable. Set specific deadlines or milestones to track your progress along the way.

By incorporating the SMART framework, you can transform broad aspirations into actionable and attainable goals. Regularly review and reassess your goals as your financial circumstances evolve. Track your progress, celebrate milestones, and make adjustments when necessary.

Interactive Exercise: Creating SMART Goals Select a financial goal and break it down using the SMART framework. Specify the amount, timeline, and action steps needed to achieve the goal.

Saving for College and Higher Education

Saving for education is an essential part of financial planning and plays a significant role in securing a brighter future. Here are some key tips to consider when saving for education:

1. **Start Early:** Time is a powerful ally when it comes to saving for education. The earlier you start, the more time your savings have to grow through the power of compound interest. By starting early, even small contributions can accumulate significantly over time.

2. **Explore Education Funding Options:** Take the time to research and explore various funding options for education. These can include scholarships, grants, work-study programs, and education loans. Scholarships and grants are free money that can help offset the cost of education, while work-study programs provide opportunities to earn money while studying. Education loans can be a viable option, but it's important to understand the terms, interest rates, and repayment options before borrowing.

3. **529 Savings Plans:** Familiarize yourself with 529 savings plans, which are tax-

advantaged investment accounts designed specifically for education expenses. These plans offer potential tax benefits and allow your savings to grow tax-free. Additionally, some states offer additional incentives, such as tax deductions or matching contributions. Research the specific benefits and eligibility criteria of 529 savings plans in your region.

4. **Set Savings Goals:** Determine how much you need to save for education by estimating the cost of tuition, fees, books, and other related expenses. Break down the total amount into manageable savings goals. Consider using online calculators or consulting with a financial advisor to help you determine an appropriate savings target.

5. **Establish a Budget:** Creating a budget can help you allocate a portion of your income specifically for education savings. Analyze your income, expenses, and financial obligations to

identify areas where you can cut back or save more. Stay disciplined and commit to consistently setting aside funds for education.

6.   **Automate Savings:** Consider setting up automatic transfers or direct deposits to a separate savings account dedicated to education. Automating your savings ensures that a portion of your income goes directly toward your education fund without requiring constant manual effort.

7.   **Regularly Review and Adjust:** As your education goals and financial circumstances change, it's important to regularly review and adjust your savings plan. Reassess your savings goals, evaluate your progress, and make necessary adjustments to stay on track.

Practical Tip: Create a budget that includes regular contributions to your education savings. Automate the process by setting up automatic transfers to your savings account.

Case Study: Emily demonstrates responsible financial planning by starting to save for college at the age of 16. Recognizing the importance of early action, she opens a 529 savings plan, a tax-advantaged investment account specifically designed for education expenses. By contributing a portion of her income from a part-time job, Emily establishes a consistent savings habit.

With the advantage of time and the compounding effect of interest, Emily's savings grow substantially over the years. The regular contributions she makes to her 529 savings plan, combined with the potential investment returns, help her accumulate a significant amount by the time she graduates from high school.

By diligently saving for college, Emily sets herself up for a more financially secure future. Her early and disciplined approach to college savings not only eases the burden of tuition expenses but also allows her to pursue her educational goals without being overwhelmed by excessive student loan debt.

Exploring Career and Education Paths

Exploring career and education paths is a vital process that allows individuals to make informed decisions about their future. By following these steps, individuals can gain clarity and set themselves up for success:

1. **Self-Assessment:** Start by conducting a thorough self-assessment to understand your interests, skills, strengths, and values. Reflect on your passions, talents, and what motivates you. This self-awareness will help you identify potential career paths that align with your personal preferences.

2. **Research Careers:** Once you have a better understanding of your interests and strengths, begin exploring different careers that match your profile. Take advantage of various resources such as career websites, job descriptions, and informational interviews to gather information about job outlook, earning potential, required qualifications, and growth opportunities. Consider the

alignment between your skills and the skills needed for each career option.

3. **Higher Education Options:** If pursuing higher education is part of your career plan, research different options available to you. Look into universities, community colleges, vocational schools, and online courses that offer programs relevant to your desired career. Consider factors such as the reputation of the institution, curriculum, faculty, cost of education, financial aid options, and the support services available to students.

Evaluate how each option aligns with your goals and preferences. Consider the curriculum's relevance to your desired career, the availability of internships or work-study opportunities, and the potential for networking and professional connections.

Interactive Exercise: Take a career assessment test or use online resources to explore different career paths. Research at least three careers that interest you and create a pros and cons list

for each. Discuss your findings with a friend or family member to gain different perspectives.

Introduction to Retirement Planning

Planning for retirement may feel distant, but starting early is crucial for ensuring a financially secure future. Here are key points to consider when it comes to retirement savings:

1. **Compound Interest:** Understand the power of compound interest. By starting to save for retirement early, you can take advantage of the compounding effect, where your investment earnings generate additional earnings over time. The longer your money remains invested, the more significant the impact of compounding.

2. **Retirement Accounts:** Familiarize yourself with retirement accounts that can help you save for retirement in a tax-efficient manner. Employer-sponsored plans, such as 401(k) or 403(b) plans, allow you to contribute a

portion of your income to a retirement account, often with the added benefit of employer matching contributions. Individual Retirement Accounts (IRAs) are another option that individuals can open independently. Understand the contribution limits, eligibility criteria, tax advantages, and investment options associated with each type of retirement account.

3. **Employer Matching Contributions:** If your employer offers a matching contribution program, take full advantage of it. Employer matching contributions are essentially free money added to your retirement account based on a percentage of your own contributions. It's wise to contribute enough to your retirement account to receive the maximum matching amount offered by your employer. Failing to do so means leaving potential retirement savings on the table.

4. **Diversify Your Investments:** Consider diversifying your retirement investments to manage risk and potentially increase returns. Depending on your risk tolerance and investment knowledge, allocate your contributions among a mix of stocks, bonds, and other investment options. Diversification helps you spread your investments across different asset classes, reducing the impact of volatility in any single investment.

5. **Regularly Review and Adjust:** Monitor your retirement savings progress regularly and make adjustments as needed. Assess your retirement goals, evaluate your investment performance, and make any necessary changes to your contributions or investment allocations. As you approach retirement age, you may need to rebalance your portfolio to reduce risk and ensure your savings align with your retirement plans.

Remember, the earlier you start saving for retirement, the more time you have to grow your investments and build a substantial nest egg. Take advantage of the power of compound interest, educate yourself on retirement account options, maximize employer matching contributions, diversify your investments, and regularly review your progress.

Practical Tip: Calculate how much you need to save for retirement and create a plan to reach your target. Consider consulting with a financial advisor to ensure you are on the right track.

Case Study: Mark understands the importance of retirement planning and takes proactive steps to secure his financial future. As soon as he becomes eligible, Mark enrolls in his employer's 401(k) plan. Recognizing the benefit of employer matching contributions, he contributes a percentage of his salary each month.

By taking advantage of the employer match, Mark effectively increases his retirement savings without any additional cost. Over time, his consistent contributions, coupled with the power of investment growth, contribute to the growth of a substantial retirement nest egg.

Mark's proactive approach to retirement planning demonstrates his commitment to long-term financial security. By starting early and maximizing the benefits offered through his employer's retirement plan, Mark is on track to enjoy a comfortable retirement.

Building Wealth and Financial Independence

Building wealth and achieving financial independence require a strategic and long-term approach. Consider implementing the following strategies to maximize your potential for success:

1. **Develop Multiple Income Streams:** Relying solely on a single source of income may limit your wealth-building potential. Explore opportunities to diversify your income by considering side businesses, freelancing, rental properties, or investments that generate passive income. By having multiple streams of income, you can

increase your overall earning potential and accelerate your wealth-building journey.

2. **Invest in Financial Education:** Continuous learning about personal finance and investing is essential for building wealth. Take the time to educate yourself about various investment vehicles, such as stocks, bonds, mutual funds, real estate, or other assets. Stay updated on market trends, investment strategies, and financial news. This knowledge will empower you to make informed decisions and seize opportunities to grow your wealth.

3. **Practice Effective Budgeting and Saving:** Budgeting remains a fundamental aspect of wealth-building. Create a comprehensive budget that prioritizes your financial goals, including saving and investing. Track your expenses, identify areas for potential savings, and allocate a portion of your income towards investments.

Regularly review and adjust your budget as necessary to ensure you stay on track.

4. **Harness the Power of Compound Interest:** Understand the concept of compound interest and use it to your advantage. By starting early and consistently contributing to investment vehicles that offer compounding, such as retirement accounts or index funds, you can benefit from the exponential growth of your investments over time. The longer your money remains invested, the greater the potential for significant wealth accumulation.

5. **Manage Debt Wisely:** Minimize high-interest debt and focus on reducing or eliminating it as part of your wealth-building strategy. Prioritize paying off debts with the highest interest rates first while making minimum payments on other debts. Avoid accumulating unnecessary debt and practice responsible borrowing when necessary.

6. **Seek Professional Guidance:** Consider consulting with a financial advisor or wealth manager to help develop a personalized wealth-building strategy. They can provide expertise, guidance, and tailored advice based on your specific financial goals and circumstances.

Interactive Exercise: Create a mock portfolio based on your risk tolerance and investment preferences. Monitor the performance of your portfolio over time.

Chapter 8: Financial Independence and Entrepreneurship

Introduction: In this chapter, we will explore the exciting world of financial independence and entrepreneurship. We'll delve into the opportunities and challenges of starting your own business and equip you with the knowledge and skills needed to succeed as an entrepreneur. Let's embark on the journey towards financial independence and entrepreneurship.

Exploring Entrepreneurial Opportunities: Embarking on the entrepreneurial journey can be an exciting and rewarding experience. To set yourself up for success, it's important to take the following steps:

1. **Identify Your Passion and Skills:** Start by exploring your interests, talents, and skills. Consider the activities that bring you joy and fulfillment. Look for areas where your expertise and knowledge

can be leveraged to create a unique business proposition. By aligning your business idea with your passion and skills, you'll be more motivated and better equipped to navigate the challenges that come with entrepreneurship.

2. **Conduct Market Research:** Before diving into your business idea, conduct thorough market research. This involves gathering information about your target audience, understanding their needs and preferences, and identifying any gaps or opportunities in the market. Evaluate the competition and assess how your offering can differentiate itself and provide value to customers. Market research helps you validate your business idea, refine your value proposition, and identify potential obstacles or challenges you may face.

3. **Develop a Business Plan:** A well-thought-out business plan serves as a roadmap for your entrepreneurial

journey. It outlines your business goals, strategies, target market, competitive analysis, and financial projections. A business plan helps you clarify your vision, make informed decisions, and secure funding if needed. It also acts as a reference point to track your progress and make adjustments along the way.

4. **Build a Strong Network:** Networking plays a vital role in entrepreneurship. Connect with like-minded individuals, industry professionals, and potential mentors who can provide guidance, support, and valuable insights. Attend networking events, join industry associations, and actively engage with online communities. Building a strong network opens doors to collaboration, partnerships, and opportunities that can accelerate the growth of your business.

5. **Secure Funding:** Determine the financial resources required to start and grow your business. Explore different funding options, such as

personal savings, loans, grants, or venture capital. Develop a clear financial plan that includes budgeting, revenue projections, and expense management. Seek professional advice if needed to ensure you have a sustainable financial foundation for your entrepreneurial venture.

6. **Take Action and Iterate:** Once you have conducted market research, developed a business plan, and secured funding, it's time to take action. Start by creating a minimum viable product (MVP) or offering your services to customers. Collect feedback, learn from your experiences, and be prepared to iterate and adapt your business strategy as you gain insights and market feedback.

7. **Embrace Continuous Learning:** Entrepreneurship is a journey of continuous learning and growth. Stay updated with industry trends, emerging technologies, and evolving customer needs. Invest in your personal and

professional development through workshops, courses, and industry conferences. Surround yourself with mentors and advisors who can provide guidance and help you navigate the challenges that arise along the way.

Practical Tip: Start small by testing your business idea on a small scale. This will help you validate your concept before making a larger commitment.

Budgeting for Business Ventures

Budgeting is a fundamental aspect of managing a business and plays a vital role in its success. To effectively budget for your business venture, consider the following tips:

1. **Start-up Costs:** Begin by identifying all the costs associated with starting your business. This includes one-time expenses like equipment purchases, leasehold improvements, initial inventory, marketing and advertising costs, legal fees, permits and licenses, and any other essential investments needed to launch your business. Create

a comprehensive list of these costs and assign estimated values to each item. This will help you develop a realistic budget and determine how much capital you need to secure.

2. **Operating Expenses:** Once your business is up and running, it's crucial to account for the ongoing operating expenses. These expenses include rent or lease payments, utilities, salaries or wages, insurance, inventory restocking, marketing and advertising campaigns, office supplies, maintenance and repairs, and any other costs required to sustain daily operations. Closely monitor your cash flow and regularly review your operating expenses to ensure that they remain within your budget.

3. **Revenue Projections:** Alongside your expenses, it's important to estimate your expected revenue or sales. Consider factors such as market demand, pricing strategies, competition, and your target customer

base. Based on these projections, you can determine whether your business is generating sufficient income to cover your expenses and achieve profitability. Be realistic in your revenue estimations and regularly track your actual performance against your projections to make necessary adjustments.

4. **Contingency Planning:** Building a contingency fund within your budget is crucial for handling unforeseen events or emergencies. Unexpected expenses or temporary revenue fluctuations can occur, and having a financial cushion can help you navigate these challenges without impacting your overall business operations. Aim to set aside a portion of your revenue or allocate specific funds towards a contingency reserve to mitigate any potential risks.

5. **Monitoring and Adjusting:** Budgeting is an ongoing process that requires regular monitoring and adjustment. Continuously track your actual income and expenses against your budgeted

amounts. Analyze any variances and identify areas where you can cut costs or allocate resources more effectively. Make informed decisions based on these insights to optimize your business's financial performance.

6. **Seek Professional Advice:** If you're new to budgeting or find it challenging to manage your business finances, consider seeking guidance from financial professionals or business advisors. They can provide expert advice on budgeting strategies, financial forecasting, and identifying potential cost-saving opportunities. Their expertise can help you make more informed financial decisions and enhance the overall financial management of your business.

Practical Tip: Set aside an emergency fund for unexpected expenses or fluctuations in revenue.

Interactive Exercise: Creating a Business Budget Create a business budget by listing all the start-up and operating expenses. Estimate

your revenue and calculate the projected profitability. Identify areas where you can reduce costs or increase revenue.

Marketing and Sales Strategies

To develop effective marketing and sales strategies for your business, consider the following key points:

1. **Define Your Target Market and Value Proposition:** Clearly identify your target market, understanding their demographics, needs, preferences, and purchasing behavior. Tailor your marketing messages and offerings to address their specific pain points and provide unique value. Define your value proposition, highlighting what sets your product or service apart from competitors and how it solves customers' problems or fulfills their desires.

2. **Establish an Online Presence:** In today's digital age, having a strong online presence is essential. Create a professional website that showcases

your products or services, provides valuable information, and offers a seamless user experience. Leverage social media platforms relevant to your target audience to engage with potential customers, share content, and build brand awareness. Consider investing in online advertising, such as pay-per-click (PPC) campaigns or social media ads, to reach a wider audience and drive targeted traffic to your website.

3. **Utilize Digital Marketing Techniques:** Take advantage of digital marketing techniques to enhance your online visibility and attract customers. Implement search engine optimization (SEO) strategies to improve your website's ranking in search engine results. Create compelling content, such as blog posts, videos, or infographics, to educate and engage your audience. Use email marketing campaigns to nurture leads and build customer loyalty. Explore influencer marketing collaborations or

partnerships with complementary businesses to expand your reach.

4. **Customer Relationship Management (CRM):** Focus on building strong relationships with your customers to foster loyalty and encourage repeat business. Provide exceptional customer service at every touchpoint, ensuring prompt and helpful responses to inquiries or concerns. Personalize the customer experience by understanding their preferences and tailoring your offerings accordingly. Implement loyalty programs, referral incentives, or exclusive offers to reward and retain your existing customer base.

5. **Monitor and Measure Results:** Regularly track and analyze your marketing and sales efforts to evaluate their effectiveness. Use analytics tools to measure website traffic, conversion rates, customer engagement, and other relevant metrics. Adjust your strategies based on data-driven insights, identifying areas for improvement and

optimizing your marketing campaigns for better results. Continuously refine your marketing and sales strategies to adapt to changing market trends and customer preferences.

Practical Tip: Leverage the power of social media influencers and online reviews to generate buzz and credibility for your business.

Case Study: Alex, a talented graphic designer, establishes his own business and utilizes social media platforms as a powerful marketing tool. He carefully curates his social media presence, showcasing his impressive portfolio and sharing captivating design content. To expand his reach, Alex collaborates with influencers who have a substantial following in the design industry. By leveraging their influence, he gains exposure to a wider audience and attracts the attention of potential clients.

Through his consistent and strategic marketing efforts, Alex's business gains momentum. His exceptional design skills and professional reputation attract high-profile clients who are impressed by his creative abilities and attention to detail. As a result, his business flourishes, and he becomes known for delivering exceptional design work that exceeds client expectations.

Alex's success in marketing his graphic design business serves as an inspiration to aspiring entrepreneurs. It highlights the importance of leveraging social media platforms, collaborating with influencers, and consistently showcasing one's skills and unique value proposition. By implementing effective marketing strategies, Alex not only increases his visibility but also establishes a strong reputation in the industry, paving the way for long-term success and growth in his business.

Financial Management for Small Businesses:

Effective financial management is essential for the success of your small business. Consider the following practices:

- Accurate Bookkeeping: Maintain detailed records of your income and expenses. Utilize accounting software or hire a professional to manage your books.

- Cash Flow Management: Monitor your cash flow closely to ensure you have enough funds to cover expenses and invest in growth opportunities.

- Pricing Strategies: Set prices that cover your costs and allow for a profit margin. Consider factors such as competition, market demand, and perceived value.

Practical Tip: Regularly review your financial statements to track the financial health of your business and identify areas for improvement.

Interactive Exercise: Cash Flow Projection Create a cash flow projection for your business, outlining your expected inflows and outflows over a specific period. Identify potential cash flow gaps and develop strategies to mitigate them.

Scaling and Growing a Business: Scaling and expanding a business is an exciting phase that requires careful planning and strategic decision-making. Once your business has established a solid foundation, you can explore various strategies to take it to the next level and reach new heights of success.

Operational efficiency plays a crucial role in scaling a business. Streamlining processes, automating tasks, and improving productivity are essential to handle increased demand without compromising on quality. By optimizing operations, you can effectively manage growth and ensure that your business can meet the demands of an expanding customer base.

Strategic partnerships can be instrumental in expanding your business reach and accessing new markets. Collaborating with complementary businesses can provide mutual benefits by tapping into each other's customer base and sharing resources. This strategic approach allows you to leverage existing networks, increase brand visibility, and open doors to new opportunities.

When considering scaling your business, funding options become important. Research different avenues such as loans, grants, or venture capital to secure the necessary capital to fuel your growth. Each funding option has its own advantages and considerations, so it's important to evaluate them based on your specific business needs and goals. By securing the right funding, you can invest in marketing, infrastructure, technology, and talent, positioning your business for expansion and success.

It's worth noting that scaling a business requires careful planning, market research, and risk assessment. While growth is an exciting prospect, it's important to have a well-thought-out strategy in place to ensure a smooth transition and sustainable growth. Continuously monitor and adapt your strategies as you scale, staying agile and responsive to market trends and customer needs.

Scaling and expanding your business are an opportunity for significant growth and increased profitability. By focusing on operational efficiency, forming strategic partnerships, and exploring funding options, you can position your business for success in new markets and propel it towards a bright and prosperous future.

Practical Tip: Continuously innovate and adapt to changing market trends to stay ahead of the competition.

Chapter 9: Financial Literacy and Beyond

In this final chapter, we will delve into advanced financial literacy topics that will empower you to take control of your financial future. We will explore the importance of continuing financial education, investment opportunities, giving back and philanthropy, maximizing tax benefits, and navigating economic challenges. Let's expand your financial knowledge and take your financial literacy to the next level.

Continuing Financial Education: Financial education is a lifelong journey. By continually expanding your knowledge, you can make informed financial decisions and stay updated on the latest trends. Consider the following strategies:

- **Reading Financial Books and Blogs:** Engage with reputable financial books, blogs, and publications to stay informed about personal finance, investing, and money management.

- **Attending Workshops and Webinars:** Participate in workshops, webinars, and seminars offered by financial experts and institutions to gain valuable insights and practical knowledge.

Practical Tip: Seek opportunities to network with professionals in the financial industry to gain valuable insights and expand your career prospects.

Exploring Investment Opportunities: As you grow your financial literacy, exploring investment opportunities becomes crucial. Consider the following tips:

- **Diversification:** Build a diversified investment portfolio by investing in different asset classes, such as stocks, bonds, mutual funds, real estate, and alternative investments.

- **Risk and Return:** Understand the relationship between risk and return. Higher-risk investments may offer higher potential returns but also carry greater risks.

- **Investment Research:** Conduct thorough research on investment options before making decisions. Consider factors such as historical performance, fees, and the underlying fundamentals of the investment.

Practical Tip: Consider investing in low-cost index funds or exchange-traded funds (ETFs) as a beginner to gain exposure to a broad range of assets.

Giving Back and Philanthropy: Giving back to the community and engaging in philanthropy can be rewarding. Consider the following strategies:

- **Identify Causes You Care About:** Reflect on social issues and causes that align with your values and interests. Research organizations and initiatives working towards those causes.

- **Volunteerism:** Explore volunteer opportunities to contribute your time and skills to organizations that address social and environmental challenges.

- **Charitable Giving:** Consider making regular donations to charitable organizations that align with your values. Research their impact and financial transparency before making contributions.

Practical Tip: Set a budget for charitable giving to ensure your contributions align with your overall financial plan.

Maximizing Tax Benefits: Understanding tax benefits can help you optimize your finances and reduce your tax burden. Consider the following strategies:

- **Retirement Contributions:** Contribute to tax-advantaged retirement accounts such as 401(k)s or IRAs to lower your taxable income and save for retirement.

- **Education Tax Credits:** Explore education-related tax credits and deductions, such as the Lifetime Learning Credit or the Student Loan Interest Deduction, to maximize tax savings while pursuing higher education.

- Itemized Deductions: Familiarize yourself with eligible itemized deductions, such as mortgage interest, medical expenses, and charitable contributions, to potentially lower your taxable income.

Practical Tip: Consult with a tax professional or use tax software to ensure you are maximizing your eligible tax benefits and deductions.

Interactive Exercise: Tax Planning Simulation Simulate different tax scenarios using tax software or online calculators. Explore how adjusting deductions and contributions impact your tax liability and overall financial situation.

Navigating Economic Challenges: Economic challenges can arise throughout your financial journey. Understanding how to navigate them is crucial. Consider the following strategies:

- Emergency Fund: Maintain an emergency fund to cover unexpected expenses and financial setbacks. Aim to save three to six months' worth of living expenses.

- **Financial Resilience:** Adopt prudent financial habits such as living within your means, avoiding excessive debt, and regularly reviewing your budget to build financial resilience.

- **Seeking Professional Advice:** During challenging economic times, consider consulting with a financial advisor who can provide guidance tailored to your specific situation.

Practical Tip: Stay informed about economic trends and news by following reputable financial publications and websites.

Remember, financial literacy is a lifelong journey, so stay curious, stay informed, and continue to grow your financial knowledge. Congratulations on completing this book, and best of luck on your financial journey ahead!

CAPITAL
DISRUPTION